Phonics Stories Long Vowels

Laurie Hunter

Illustrated by Gabrielle Watson

Published by Laurie Hunter
Austin

Phonics Stories, Long Vowels
Copyright © 2020 Laurie Hunter

Companion Instruction Manual: *Cultivating Reading and Phonics Skills, 1st Grade – 3rd Grade by Laurie Hunter*
Companion Phonics Storybooks by Laurie Hunter with Illustrations:
Phonics Stories - Short Vowels - Level 1
Phonics Stories - Long Vowels - Level 2
Phonics Stories - The Other Vowel Sounds - Level 3
Phonics Stories - Advanced Long and Short Vowel Patterns - Level 4

For inquiries and to obtain permission, please submit a written request to
Laurie Hunter, 9009 Corran Ferry Dr. Austin, TX 78749
www.lauriehunter.org

Library of Congress Cataloguing-in-Publication Data

Hunter, Laurie
Phonics Stories, Long Vowels/ Hunter, Laurie; Illustrated by Gabrielle Watson
ISBN 978-0-9974882-6-5

1. Reading. 2. Phonics. 3. Phonetic method - Study and teaching (elementary).
4. English language - Orthography and spelling. I. Laurie Hunter. II. Phonics Stories, Long Vowels

372.46 H 2021   2021919720

Publisher: Laurie Hunter
Cover Design: Bojan/Pixelstudio
Cover and Interior Illustrations: Gabrielle Watson
Interior Design: Ramona Andrea Făgăraş
Printed in the United States of America

Level 2: For intermediate readers, all ages, all abilities

Guided Reading Level: E - I

CHAPTER 1 | **THE BEAST**

I dream of a beast.
I dream of a beast in the sea.

I scream!
I scream, and it leaps!

It leaps and weeps.

I feel sad for the beast.

I speak to him in the dream.

He tells me his name is Steve.
He is sweet.

I was a creep.
I was a creep to scream.

He is not a beast.
Who is the beast? Me.

Instructors, you have the option to preview the following words with students before they attempt reading the story. Also, students should practice spelling some of the words after reading each story.

Long e e says its name	Long e ea vowel team	Long e ee vowel team	Long e e_e vowel team	Short e sounds like elephant
the	dream	weep	Steve	tell
he	beast	feel		
me	sea	meet		
	scream	sweet		
	leaps	creep		
	speak			

Introduce the Literary Elements to Students
1) Who is the main character?
2) What is the conflict?
3) What is the resolution?
4) What is the theme?

 Answers:
1) The main character is the girl who is dreaming.
2) To find the conflict, you can ask, "What problem is the main character having?"

   The girl sees an octopus in her dream. She fears it's a beast and screams, and that made the octopus feel sad.
3) To find the resolution, you can ask, "How was the problem solved?"

She feels bad for hurting Steve's feelings, and she speaks to him. She discovers that he is not a beast. She realizes she was a beast for over-reacting.

4) To find the theme you can ask, "What is the lesson the author wants the character or reader to learn?"

There is usually more than one theme.

Here are some themes from this story:

Sometimes people are not as scary as we think.

If we hurt someone's feelings, we can make them feel better.

When we meet someone new or different, we should not judge them.

Don't overreact or be dramatic.

Can you think of other possible themes?

CHAPTER 2 | **I CAN RIDE NINE BIKES AT ONE TIME**

I can ride.

I can ride nine bikes.
I can ride nine bikes at one time!

I lied.
I tried to ride nine bikes at one time.
I died!

I lied.
I did not die.

I tried to ride nine bikes at one time and I *almost* died.

So I ride five bikes at one time, and I am fine!

Instructors, you have the option to preview the following words with students before they attempt reading the story. Also, students should practice spelling some of the words after reading each story.

Long i i says its name	Long i ie vowel team	Long i i_e vowel team	Short i sounds like igloo
I	lied	ride	did
	tried	nine	
	die	bikes	
	died	time	
		yikes!	
		five	
		fine	

Introduce the Literary Elements to Students

1) Who is the main character?
2) What is the conflict?
3) What is the resolution?
4) What is the theme?

Answers:

1) The main character is Steve, the octopus, who can ride bikes.

2) To find the conflict, you can ask, "What problem is the main character having?"

   The octopus lied saying he can ride nine bikes at the same time. Then he said he died trying to ride nine bikes.

3) To find the resolution, you can ask, "How was the problem solved?"

The octopus told the truth that he tried to ride nine bikes and almost died. So now, he rides only five bikes at the same time.

4) To find the theme you can ask, "What is the lesson the author wants the character or reader to learn?"

There is usually more than one theme.

Here are some themes from this story:

Don't lie. But if you do, tell the truth like Steve did.

We should think about safety before we try something that may be dangerous.

Can you think of other possible themes?

CHAPTER 3 | **SPAIN**

One day, Steve set sail.
One day, Steve set sail to Spain.

In Spain, he takes a train to a trail.

He takes the trail to a cave.
In the cave, he is lost.
Steve gets his map.

With the map, he makes his way.
He makes his way in the cave.

In the cave, he sees shapes (formations):
a brain, tail, snake, and snail!

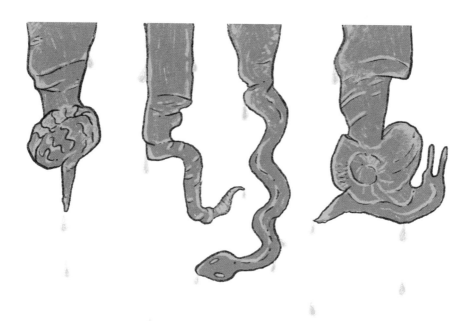

Rain water made its way to the cave and made the shapes.
The rain water made the brain, tail, snake, and snail.
It was amazing!

Instructors, you have the option to preview the following words with students before they attempt reading the story. Also, students should practice spelling some of the words after reading each story.

Long a a	Long a ay	Long a ay	Long a a_e	Short a
says its name	vowel team	vowel team	vowel team	sounds like apple
a	day	Spain	takes	map
for-ma-tions	way	sail	cave	and
a-ma-zing		train	makes	
		trail	shapes	
		brain	snake	
		tail	made	
		snail		
		rain		

Introduce the Literary Elements to Students
1) Who is the main character?
2) What is the conflict?
3) What is the resolution?
4) What is the theme?

Answers:
1) The main character is Steve, the octopus, who sailed to Spain.
2) To find the conflict, you can ask, "What problem is the main character having?"

   Steve gets lost in the cave.
3) To find the resolution, you can ask, "How was the problem solved?"

Steve remembers his map. By bringing a map, Steve has come prepared. His travels lead him to find amazing cave formations.

4) To find the theme you can ask, "What is the lesson the author wants the character or reader to learn?"

There is usually more than one theme.

Here are some themes from this story:

You can travel and see interesting things.

Nature can create amazing wonders.

Being prepared keeps you safe.

Can you think of other possible themes?

CHAPTER 4 | **HOME**

Steve likes to roam.
Steve roams the globe.
He drove a boat.
He drove a boat to the coast
of Mexico.

On the coast of Mexico, he saw
beautiful beaches.

On the coast, he saw homes of
Mayans that lived long ago.

He swam with beautiful fish and saw their homes of coral.

He saw beautiful mangrove trees.
Mangrove trees are home to so
many animals and fish.
The mangrove trees clean the
water and air.

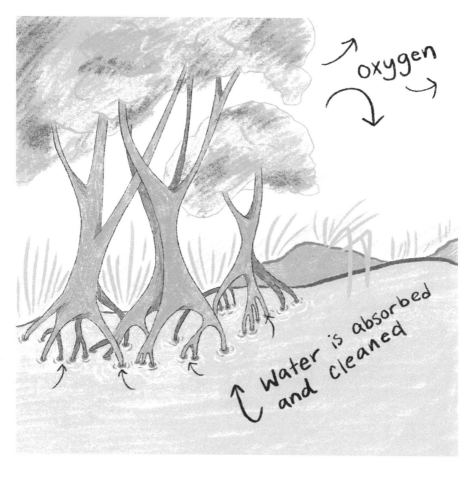

Steve had fun, but he hopes to go
back to his home!

Instructors, you have the option to preview the following words with students before they attempt reading the story. Also, students should practice spelling some of the words after reading each story.

Long o o says its name	Long o oa vowel team	Long o o_e vowel team	Short o sounds like ○ctopus
Mex-i-co a-go so go	roam boat coast	home globe drove mangrove hope	on

Introduce the Literary Elements to Students

1) Who is the main character?
2) What is the conflict?
3) What is the resolution?
4) What is the theme?

 Answers:

1) The main character is Steve, the octopus, who drove a boat to Mexico.
2) To find the conflict, you can ask, "What problem is the main character having?"

    There is not much of a conflict, is there? Steve drove a boat and swam in the ocean, which could have been dangerous. But they weren't much of a problem.
3) To find the resolution, you can ask, "How was the problem solved?"

Steve's travels lead him to find ancient Mayan homes, coral, and mangrove trees.

4) To find the theme you can ask, "What is the lesson the author wants the character or reader to learn?"

There is usually more than one theme.

Here are some themes from this story:

You can travel and see interesting things.

Mangrove trees are homes for animals, and these unique trees clean the water and air.

Can you think of other possible themes?

CHAPTER 5 | **THE FLU**

Steve was sick.
Steve was sick with the flu.

His doctor was Dr. Sue.
Dr. Sue took care of Steve.

Steve had to be in a cube.
He had to be in a cube, so others
did not get his flu.

Steve had a cute blue mask.
Dr. Sue gave him fruit juice.
The fruit juice was blue too.

Soon, Steve felt better.
No more flu!
No more cube!

Steve gave Dr. Sue a huge
"Thank You!"
He still uses cute blue masks
and washes his hands often.
How about you?

Instructors, you have the option to preview the following words with students before they attempt reading the story. Also, explain to students that they may not have studied the phonics rules for the words on the right, so they may not know how to pronounce those words yet. Be prepared to read the words on the right for the students during the story. Also, students should practice spelling some of the words after reading each story.

Long u u says its name	Long u ue vowel team	Long u ui vowel team	Long u u_e vowel team	Long u We'll learn these later!
flu	Sue blue	fruit juice	cube cute huge uses	achoo! too soon you

Introduce the Literary Elements to Students
1) Who is the main character?
2) What is the conflict?
3) What is the resolution?
4) What is the theme?

Answers:
1) The main character is Steve, the octopus.
2) To find the conflict, you can ask, "What problem is the main character having?"
   Steve was sick with the flu.
3) To find the resolution, you can ask, "How was the problem solved?"

Steve went to the doctor, and she made him feel better. He wears a mask and washes his hands, so he doesn't get sick again. He was thankful.

4) To find the theme you can ask, "What is the lesson the author wants the character or reader to learn?"

There is usually more than one theme.

Here are some themes from this story:

When we get sick, sometimes we need the help of a doctor.

We can take steps to prevent others from getting sick.

We can take steps to prevent ourselves from getting sick again.

Can you think of other possible themes?

CHAPTER 6 | **MICE IN THE CITY**

Steve misses his friends.
His friends are mice.
The mice live in the city.

Steve rides his bike to see the mice.
The mice ride on his bicycle.
They ride his bicycle in the big city.

They ride his bike to the gym.
Steve and the mice dance in
gym class.
They dance and prance.

After gym class, they like to eat. The mice eat rice and ice cream. Yum!

After eating rice and ice cream,
they dance again.
It puts a smile on their face.

It is nice to dance and eat
ice cream with friends!

Instructors, you have the option to preview the following words with students before they attempt reading the story. Soft c and g can be difficult. While students read the story, be prepared to help them read some of the words below. Also, students should practice spelling some of the words after reading each story.

c hard c	ce soft c	ci soft c	cy soft c	gy soft g
class	mice	city	bicycle	gym
cream	dance			
	prance			
	rice			
	ice			
	face			
	nice			

Introduce the Literary Elements to Students

1) Who is the main character?
2) What is the conflict?
3) What is the resolution?
4) What is the theme?

Answers:

1) The main character is Steve.
2) To find the conflict, you can ask, "What problem is the main character having?"

   Steve misses his friends.
3) To find the resolution, you can ask, "How was the problem solved?"

Steve rides his bike to see his friends. He dances, eats ice cream, and has fun with his friends.

4) To find the theme you can ask, "What is the lesson the author wants the character or reader to learn?"

There is usually more than one theme.

Here are some themes from this story:

It's good to spend time with friends.

If you miss someone, you can try to see them.

Being active with friends is fun.

Can you think of other possible themes?

GET TO KNOW THE AUTHOR AND ILLUSTRATOR

Laurie Hunter has been teaching children of all ages and abilities how to read and resolve conflicts in everyday life, since 2005. She teaches students how reading strengthens our problem-solving abilities. By identifying conflicts, resolutions, and themes, we can see how other people solve problems - or not! Laurie aims to inspire children and teens to creatively triumph over life's challenges. Her favorite sea creature is the octopus, of course!

Gabrielle Watson is a multidisciplinary artist with a BFA from the Cleveland Institute of Art, where she studied Biomedical Illustration. She loves utilizing her creative talents to help support learning and all kinds of educational adventures. Her favorite type of sea creatures are nudibranchs because they look like sea caterpillars!